How to Attract Money

The Simple Guide to Getting Money

(Powerful Manifestation Techniques to Attract Wealth)

Robert Criswell

Published By **Chris David**

Robert Criswell

*How to Attract Money: The Simple Guide to
Getting Money (Powerful Manifestation
Techniques to Attract Wealth)*

ISBN   978-1-990373-88-6

No part of this guidebook shall be reproduced in any form without permission in writing from the publisher except in the case of brief quotations embodied in critical articles or reviews.

Legal & Disclaimer

Table Of Contents

Chapter 1: Having Money

Be sure to follow the laws of God for money

If you look at the success tales of millionaires across all around the world, you'll find that regardless of whether they come coming from Europe or any other nation, regardless of whether they're young or old and at some point, they have all been following the same pattern in order to attain their wealth. One of the most important financial laws is the fact that it attracts by people who cherish and appreciate money. We have explained in the introduction paragraphs, you shouldn't consider money to be an issue that is the "root for all the problems" according to the statements made by the majority of us who live in our world. However, if you take the time to look closely at the lives of these people, you'll find that their cash flow is restricted. So, respecting money is the in the first place to generate more money in your life.

In the book "Power of your Sub-Conscious mind" written by Joseph Murphy, it is said that imaginative visualization holds the power of awe to increase the financial well-being of. By energizing your subconscious mind with positive and exact thoughts of prosperity is certain to be realized in the form of you'll have access to the wealth of infinity. The book also reveals emotions and thoughts that bring about anxiety, poverty and misery can be a hindrance to your financial well-being.

When you understand that universal principle of financial law, you are able to reap the greatest benefits of it. It is a constant connection with your mind's subconscious. Whatever you put into your mind is a reality within your everyday existence. As an example, if you grow paddy, it is impossible to harvest maize. This is the same principle applies to the moral law regarding money. If you fill your mind with thoughts about difficulties, suffering and poverty then you won't be able to reap the fruits of riches. This will result in those same negative experiences in your daily life through experiences. To achieve wealth through the law of attraction to money, it is important to understand that your thoughts are acting as a tyrannical servant. It does not care whether your mind is working toward your goals, it just follows the instructions you give it. To achieve this, you must train your brain to use the universality of money to help you achieve financial prosperity. Techniques for energizing your mind's subconscious to achieve the financial rewards you have set are described in the following sections.

The plants of prosperity, abundance potential, and plenitude in your head to be to manifest in the variety of experiences in your life. Believe in this divine law, which propels you toward the success you desire. If you are a believer in it, you will be able to make miraculous changes within your own life. It is important to have faith within yourself will be explored in the following article.

Create unlimited thought

If you're still trying to reach the level of financial success you want It is the perfect the time to start developing an unlimited thought process. This will cost you nothing, yet will give you a lot. Even though you know that you've still not achieved the status of financial success You should shift your mindset to that one of an eminent millionaire. While it might sound odd psychologically, it's a good way to remove you from negative thoughts about poverty or lack of confidence. insecurity and despair that have a negative effect on your finances every day. The consciousness of the universe is endless. The same is the inner awareness. The key is to recognize the universal law of physics and toss all negative thoughts that hinder your mind and block your way to achieving financial success. Let your mind loose and allow yourself to imagine living your dream lifestyle by imagining it. If this unending thinking is embedded in your consciousness the unlimited force of nature makes the universe manifest in your existence. So, it is essential to think about possibilities and not limit yourself. You are free to consider your ideas in a limitless manner and relish the benefits of the universal mind.

Unlimited thinking is the act of daily fantasies until you can experience the dream as reality. There is no limit to how you think about this. The first step is to consider what you desire to achieve in your life. You should then give up to the infinite possibilities of your mind and take in the joy in the way it's already been achieved. It is not impossible to achieve anything in the realm of your imagination. So, you're free to grow and develop your infinite thoughts and fill your head with feelings of achievement until they actually come your direction. Don't allow space in your thoughts for sadness losses, limits, or shortage. This is useless and only it exacerbates your pain.

Believe in yourself and make wonders

If you are a believer in your own self, you may be surprised by what happens throughout your day-to-day life. There are a lot of books on the topic of how to attract the money. It's all nothing if you do not have confidence in yourself enough to try the techniques. A mere theoretical understanding is nothing more than cash in a bank account cannot be withdrawn. If you've got belief in the power of God to make you rich, then you're on the right track to financial prosperity.

It is a useful tool to use in your life. When you believe in yourself your universal consciousness is in your favor. Utilizing universal laws but not trusting in your own abilities is like filling an empty container with water. It is possible in your quest to get there but you won't be able to step even a centimeter forward. If you're not stable enough to trust the power of your abilities and doubt your power to the world, it isn't possible to benefit from this. Believers are a key factor in drawing money toward your. If your present situation doesn't satisfy your needs, then you should believe you can improve the way you live and increase your wealth as you wish. It is within you, even if you aren't conscious of it. If you remain stuck in your squalid circumstances and do not have the confidence to move from it and move on, you'll be within the same place the rest of your life. If you wish to benefit from the universal law that allows you to attract cash, self-confidence is required to be instilled into your brain. If you can do this and you are able to see for yourself the miracles that happen within your own daily life.

Make your life more clear, joyful and light through money

To attract more money, you must also be able how to utilize it with clarity happiness, enthusiasm and joy. The act of spending money is a aspect of this. This doesn't mean that you have to spend every maximum amount. However, the ultimate outcome in attracting funds should be your happiness. Holding on to each penny that you earn is the result of self-deception that you do not have enough funds. It is a negative emotion that triggers desire and increases the distance between you and the proper measure of riches. However, you must make money, with the goal of creating happiness in your life. So, it's vital to be aware of the value of what you earn. If you want to benefit from the wealth that surrounds you efficiently, you need to understand the goal in earning money.

It is an old adage that is popular among a few people that money cannot buy happiness. It is true in a glance, however there's another side to the coin. It is possible that you will not be able to walk into the mall to shop, or spend cash and purchase happiness. Many things that related to your happiness can be achieved through cash. Imagine you'd like to embark on an international excursion with the best of your buddies. It is your dream to stay with them in comfortable and warm apartments while enjoying delicious food items. You would like to experience new adventures of exploring unexplored places and experience new exciting adventures. I'm sure as you're studying these articles, you are likely to be excited by the joy and experience the experience will bring. This is joy, which you will experience by spending no the money. This is merely an illustration of how money affects our happiness in a significant amount.

The money we have is neither good nor good or bad. The only thing that matters is what people do with it. Take the example of charities that assist the most vulnerable people in all over the globe. They make smiles appear on many faces. It is a great instance of using money to create the power of light. It is also a proof to prove that money is a light source in the lives of people if it is used in an improved course.

Follow your intuition

For attracting money to live an enjoyable life, you should take note of your own direction. This is a crucial element to tap into the wealth of riches. When you're feeling down or depressed and depressed, you may unconsciously seek out someone for an opinion or support. However, if you trust more in yourself more than any other person on the planet, you are more likely to trust your own voice. Instead of seeking comfort from the outside, you should look within for the source of your inner peace. Every one of us is blessed with an inner counselor which will never cause us to become needy.

Based on the understanding of your personal adviser, you are able to communicate with it to find out what amount of money you'll need to live your life according to your mind. In turn, your intuition will help you decide the right path for achieving your financial ambitions. Prior to listening to your own brain, you should be calm and peaceful. If your brain is occupied in trying to figure out quick solutions to ease the burden of your finances Your inner thoughts won't have time to help you. It is therefore crucial to examine yourself and get rid of the chaos of your brain to make the most benefit. When your thoughts are calm and calm, it will surely show your the most efficient approach to achieving your objectives. The ability to listen to your own inner voice is more effective than looking to a counselor or adviser because nobody knows your strengths, weaknesses and flaws better than your mind. So, get your mind into an unwinding state, and then listen to it in order to get the most effective guidance in attracting the money you want.

Make use of advanced manifesting methods

Millionaires and wealthy individuals all over the world, conscious or not, are employing sophisticated manifesting strategies to reach their goals. If you apply these sophisticated strategies and the law of attracting cash, a flood of wealth can be generated throughout your daily life.

Paying gratitude and visualization can be seen as a highly effective manifestation technique to attract the money. Visualization with creativity has the ability to create wealth. If, for instance, you wish to earn huge amounts of cash and have a luxurious lifestyle, it is possible to create the mental picture that you're living in a lavish home with stunning interior design. It is as if you're driving your car of dreams.

It can also be described as a daydream. Scientists have discovered that daydreaming has the potential to transform our lives since the motivation behind it could be ignored. When you visualize the future life that you desire, you must acknowledge your subconscious mind's role in creating the space for you to live the life that you want. Always remember to show the subconscious mind a thank you.

In the book, "The power of your Sub-Conscious Mind" your subconscious mind must be filled with positive visuals that allow the person to perceive themselves as and prosperous. The book further states that the ideal time for adolescent re-infusing our sub conscious mind is during the time that we're about to fall asleep as well as when we've just gotten up. Research has shown that in those times, the subconscious mind can be able to comprehend any sensation that is injected by the mind. So, it is important to be feeding your mind during these moments of the day, expecting positive responses from your subconscious mind. You can speak to your inner self with a prayer. You can convince yourself of how fortunate you are to be able to access these avenues of cash and have money coming in day after day. If you continue to store these thoughts into your subconscious mind during times when your mind's subconscious is engaged, the power of your mind's subconscious will be able to answer your prayers quickly.

Also, you should switch the mentality that you are "wanting money" with the mentality to "having money". The thing is, we don't attract things that we would like, but we are able to draw attention to what we already are able to attract with what we have. Thus, you should adopt a mindset that you have funds. This may be a difficult task to you if your brain is consumed by feelings of insufficiency and limitations. This challenge is however overcome if you are able changing the direction of thought. Start with a basic practice to help train your brain to view you as a successful person imagine the sheer number of people who have ability to access computers and the internet? Yet, there are billions of people who may not even have ever experienced the computer. You may also have mobile phones as well as access to the internet, but these are far distant dreams for many people around the world. Thinking this way can aid you in regaining from being viewed as someone who is less fortunate. If you can develop an outlook that you have money and earning it, you'll attract more wealth.

Make your dream work a reality

In order to attract cash, an active and balanced lifestyle plays an important role. If you do not have an organized schedule for your routine and routine, it could be easy to spend your time doing nothing and have a direct effect on your ability to stay focused from your financial objectives. In order to make your life a success make sure you incorporate time for relaxation into your daily schedule. It is also crucial to limit the tasks that take up a lot of your energy and time. Also, you should be thinking over your daily errands in order to avoid further hassles. People who don't have an organized schedule for their jobs, end up stuck at a particular level. They stagnate and miss out on many opportunities that might be beneficial financially. This is why it's crucial to make a change. While people love to make a lot of money, but not everyone can are able to earn money in a short time. People work throughout the day and get receive a low salary. This is a sign that while people shouldn't feel exhausted, working on your own isn't enough to draw in money. Be aware that some relaxation can help you reenergize your enthusiasm. If you plan your work correctly, this will result in you attracting an increase in income.

Rethink your assumptions, and you will be able to achieve you to achieve

If you're not happy by your financial situation today, or have a hard time buying items you desire There must be an overhaul of your mindset. It is best to take some period of time to evaluate yourself and discover what you've missed. No matter how at it and are moving forward, it is time to modify your actions and thoughts. This should begin by shifting your views. Do not allow yourself to be influenced by opinions that could hinder you to make cash. Many people are of the idea that getting money is just a matter of luck, which is believed to be a privilege by a small portion of the world. The truth is, there are only a handful of people that believe in the spiritual laws of money as well as the ability of their subconscious mind to attract money. If they believe in these principles that they can be entitled to receive it. Other people may consider it an act of luck or the hand of God. In the beginning, God can be found in you in the event that you alter your thinking and let success happen. The mind that is focused on positive thoughts promises to bring happiness to your life.

Use magnets and draw on your the thing you'd like to achieve

You own your riches. You are not the boss or customer who determines what amount of money you ought to have. Your choice is completely yours in regards to the amount of money you would like to bring to you. If you've chosen to draw this amount of money, there's a method to draw it toward you. Visualization as mentioned above is a effective method of attracting cash towards you. To reap the greatest benefits of this technique, you must create visuals that appear that are as authentic as you can. It is important to feel that you already have the prosperity you wish to bring to you. Think as vividly as you possibly can until it is a tangible sensation for you. It is also possible to imagine your self as a source of energy with power radiating around yourself, as if you were an electric magnet. It is also possible to imagine the coil that starts from you moves all around your. The length of the coil could be visualized according to your desire to instill into you with. The coil of your imagination will surround the person you are spreading your strength throughout and drawing in whatever you'd like, which includes cash.

This can be used in a way to discover the wealth of luck that is waiting for you.

Chapter 2: Best Ways To Spend Money Wisely

Create a Budget

In terms of your financial success, it's a good idea to keep an eye on the fact that spending the money you have wisely is in tandem to attracting the money. If you're not mindful when making purchases, money is more likely to be distracted instead of being attracted. In order to make sure you spend money in a responsible manner, avoiding the unnecessary expenditures, adhering according to an established budget is the most practical method. When you make an budget, you gain the control of your hard-earned cash. This puts you in a position in which you are the one who controls your finances and not the money that is controlling your life. The process also allows you to stay in the present and focused on your financial success. This is crucial if have limited funds. This will help you save money by not spending it on items that aren't serving your financial needs. When you're focussed on your financial objectives, you're most likely to concentrate on these goals. This will help you avoid excessive expenditure.

It also provides you with an understanding of what you spend your money on. If you are prone to spending the cash on items and services on a whim in a blind spot, you could be spending a significant amount of dollars without even knowing. If you're spending in line with a budget, you are aware of the amount you are spending your money on. Therefore, you are able to adjust your expenses on a daily basis to profit you financially. The process also offers the benefit of keeping track of your money and saving which are crucial in order to control your money flow and future financial needs. Also, it demonstrates what money is working for you ahead of time. If you're working to a budget, then you may also save money to cover your expenses in case of emergency. If you don't, you are likely to use every dollar that is available. If you're involved the financial affairs of someone other than yourself, it's crucial to establish a budget since it affects the way you allocate your money. In the case of paying for your spouse, putting together a budget, let each be aware of how much money you are spending on.

If you're spending your funds in line with a budget, it allows you to anticipate your financial position to come in the future. This will provide you with cautions prior to jumping into the actual problem. It can also tell you when you're in a situation to obtain the loan. This will help you understand your current situation and allows for a viable financial position that you can maintain in the future. It also allows you to generate extra cash since it doesn't make the process of paying the bills. This saves your from having to pay fines, penalties and late fees as well as charges. In the end, it means you have additional money in your account.

You can plan your purchases ahead of time

If you can plan your purchases ahead of time, you will get an even better deal. This lets you shop for what's most important to your needs. If you make a list of your purchases prior to going into the mall or grocery store by making a list of items you want to purchase and save your time and cash. A pre-planned shopping list lets you buy the items you want according to your preferences. If for instance, you plan to go to the mall on a Sunday. If this is the case that you make a list of your shopping needs throughout the week prior to the weekend. After that, based on what's listed in your shopping checklist, you'll know where to go purchasing your products. Once you've got an idea of what you'll need during the weekend, you could look for places that offer the most affordable price for the items you want to purchase. If you are planning your purchases prior to the time you need it, you'll can also take the time to find the most reputable stores to visit. Pew scheduled shopping will also save your from impulse buys. So, even if get enticed by items that are not listed on your schedule, you may be able to carry it to your next time you shop. It stifles your impulses, which can lead you to spend more than you want. If you can plan your purchases ahead of time, you will have money on to cover any emergency. There is no need to be spending excessively or without reason. You are conscious of the worth of your hard-earned cash.

Do not buy impulse items

The word itself implies that impulse purchases are impulse purchases that are taken with no prior understanding or information. This is an impulse purchase which can result in a huge loss of your cash. You could call it an error you're taking while you shop since it has a number of negative consequences for your finances. With your natural tendency to make purchasing on impulse, many stores nowadays strategically place products near to the counter, with a goal at attracting your attention to these items. As part of their marketing strategy, they often store their products in a manner that's eye-catching to draw you in. If you're convinced to buy one of these items, even though you do actually need they at present You are enticed by the marketing tactics they employ. Success of their advertising strategies in the opposite way can lead to an impulse purchase, which may be a waste of your cash. When you're purchasing, be aware that there shouldn't be place for impulse purchases when you truly want to draw cash.

There are no limits to our desires However, the cash we have in our pockets is not unlimited. This is why it is important to make use of the limited sum of money efficiently. It is common to purchase something on impulse believing it will bring you joy. However, this doesn't occur often. If you decide to buy something on an instant without considering it and it is a pleasant purchase, but however only for a few minutes. You are then shocked when you realise that you've wasted money that could have gone to on something else. It's far too tardy. In the future, you may think that the product that you purchased hastily might not be as crucial in the way you thought it was.

The impulse buying prevents the possibility of achieving your goals. The purchase keeps you from your dreams. In the end, you're lost and lose focus. Imagine you are about to make a payment to graduate school. When you get to the college there is a stunning outfit. The dress is so appealing that you decide to purchase this dress with the funds you've set aside for your study. The purchase you made on impulse provided you with a stunning outfit with temporary pleasure however, you are stuck for a year before you can get back to school. It is a straightforward way to illustrate how impulse purchases eat away the wealth of your life in a wasteful manner. So, if you're attracted to something you love without thinking about it be sure to keep yourself from thinking about the true value of what you are buying. The self-control you have to maintain is to keep your preferences in check and think critically about the financial implications. When you are out shopping then you are aware there are a lot of products that are available for that will satisfy you. However, you should bear in mind that you may not have enough money to spend it all. So, it is best to put aside the impulse buys and make space for your priorities. Remember to think before taking a leap!

Shop by yourself

Some individuals think shopping can be a necessity, but to others it's an activity or even a mode of expression. Many people go out to get things in the event that shopping becomes a necessity for their needs. However, some individuals, and mostly women are more likely to join a person while they go for a shopping trip. It isn't a good option if your focus is on earning the cash. A single purchase can yield benefits in a variety of ways.

When you shop on your own and you're shopping on your own, you're a free bird. There is enough time for you to explore and decide prior to making a purchase. There may be a limit to your choice to walk in the case of someone else along with you. They might not want to spend some time on the street until you have found the ideal option that is right for you. In this moment it is possible to be influenced to select the second option. It could be financially detrimental to you.

The solitude of shopping usually, it keeps your from making impulse purchases. If you're shopping with a friend they might influence you to buy something that may not be essential to you. Additionally, when the person you are shopping with is making purchases, they could entice you to purchase identical items. In human nature, these kinds of situations happen naturally. So, by recognizing your desires, you should be aware of situations that negatively impact your financial situation. Also, you won't have a possibility to judge your purchases against other items. This means you're totally in control of your spending budget. If you notice that your partner spends more than you do, there is a possibility that you're making a purchase for your own image. This kind of nonsense can cause a costly buying spree.

If you're shopping together with someone, the experience of buying presents itself as a leisure activity instead of a necessity. In the end, you're enticed by visit a food outlet even if you're really hungry, paving the way for a costly expense. Shopping alone can save the person from these problems. So, try enjoying your the shopping experience in solitude.

Beware of marketing

The role of marketers is to market their product. They make a demand for us, and then make us want to purchase the product. It's called marketing. In this area it is their use of techniques and language to entice clients. If you are able to be influenced by them it is a risk with regards to your finances. Allow marketers to do their work. You control your choices. They can't affect your budget until you allow them to affect your wallet. So, it is important to think about your requirements and reach the conclusion that you do not require a product, even although they're promoting it, the product, you are required to purchase it. artificial need that they have created that they have created for you. As an example, Coca-Cola is a beverage that is consumed in many regions of the globe. The moment Coca-Cola first came into Asia the company promoted it as a drink that could be consumed after eating rice. It was a huge commercial success, and it's been deemed a necessity. However, it was never an essential requirement. However, now it's ingrained within the heads of consumers that a meal would be insufficient without Coca-Cola. If you don't allow room to these desires created by marketing, you'll have financial consequences.

In the supermarkets, you'll encounter promotional teams, who promote various kinds of services and goods. They will meet with you individually and show you the advantages of their merchandise. In these instances, it is important to take care of what they say. Sometimes, they

If you're tempted to purchase something based on the ideas generated by advertising, be sure to ask yourself if you actually need it, and whether it's is worth spending the money on it. Be sure to think about it several times before jumping into a rash decision, as they cost your cash.

Keep an eye out for sales and discounts

If you're an avid shopaholic, be taking a crucial shopping trick into consideration. It is possible to save money by shopping more efficiently in the event that you're waiting on discount sales or discounts. Nearly all shops offer discounts and sales to its customers in the holiday season. Clearance sales on stock are another an element of the deal. When you shop at these stores, you can buy several items at the exact amount that you would spend on a couple of things.

It is important to be patient until these benefits become available. As an example, the month of December is the month of celebration across the globe. This time of year, numerous stores selling textiles and food markets provide special discounts for the customers they serve. Also, they offer substantial discounts to its clients. If you shop during November in the month, this is a shrewd choice you take. It is better to wait for discount sales and sales to conserve money could be used for a purchase you value more. your needs.

Do your research

It is essential to research your options before you purchase. Nowadays, there's huge competition among marketing companies and all advertise their services and products as top-quality of their variety. The use of exaggeration is a significant aspect of the tale. This can be confusing with regards to what you must choose. If you want to make the right purchase, make sure you be thorough. This will allow you to make purchases that will never be regretted.

If you make purchases in haste and without thinking, you're more susceptible to regret and anxiety. This could result in wasting funds. In the event that you're not happy with your purchase then you'll have replace it, which will require additional funds. In other words, you'll need to purchase an item that will consume the majority of your cash in vain. If you're unhappy with the product you purchase, you're provided with the option of reselling the item within a specific duration. You can't swap it out for something that comes at a cheaper price. The item should be at the same amount or greater. However, if you purchase it after doing a sufficient amount of research you will not have need for exchanges or additional expenses.

You are now easily able to connect to the information you need. So the more companies elevate their offerings, the more exposure you have to the environment in which it is possible to judge its legitimacy. Internet is an effective tool that allows you to examine the quality of the product you will purchase. It is always possible to conduct review the pros and cons before making purchase. Make sure you have enough time for this research in order to prevent any from having to worry about the future. Also, you can talk to individuals who have previously utilized the product or service, and ask for their opinions. This is an extremely practical method to evaluate the value of something based on what they find through the experience of a first-hand user. Often, the exact product can be found at various price points in different locations. If you are making an online purchase, the cost could be than the price you pay. If you're conducting a comparison research, you are able to examine the prices of items in a single transaction.

If you purchase after conducting study, it will reward you with a variety of benefits. In essence, it allows the buyer to use their money very effectively. You will be happy knowing that the money you spent was used in the most efficient way within the budget you have set. Also, it saves you funds that you're supposed to use on the streets and fumbling around the shops. If you are in the habit of researching before making a purchase, it might lead to you attracting cash.

All costs should be taken into the account

If you are able to take all costs into account, then you will be able to handle your finances more effectively. It provides you with a clear image of the way you used the cash. This is a way to can help you to manage your finances. It can greatly benefit you when you keep the practice of logging your daily costs. You will be able to easily get complete details of all your costs at the close of each month. If you track each penny that comes in or out of your pockets, it could be financially beneficial in the longer time.

The tracking of your expenses provides insights into how money moves through and exits your life. You no longer feel that money is in control however, you're still with a position that you have control over your money. Take receipts for all the things you purchase. This makes it easier to keep up-to-date your journal by recording all your earnings as well as your expenditure.

Give yourself occasional, inexpensive treat

If you're concerned regarding your financial situation You are more intent on securing the money you have. This doesn't mean your money is treated differently than the other ones you have. The reason you want to attract cash is to enjoy your lifestyle without a trace of sorrow. This is why treating yourself to a better standard is vital. Offering yourself a regular, low-cost treats is the ideal method to achieve this. You will get the feeling that you're earning enough to support your family and not doing it to make the money. The concept of a treat every now and then is a variety of varieties. You could buy an outfit and be satisfied. Go to a restaurant for a meal and enjoy something unique to please yourself. You can also meet a new friend. The trick is convincing yourself that you need to use your money spent to get an improved life. If you are able to save the money, your ultimate goal will be to gain an improved living.

Chapter 3: Extra Money Makes

Can Money Buy Happiness?

The money you spend will not buy happiness. It's not just an issue of visiting an establishment and buying the money. We can however spend our money to purchase things that contribute to our satisfaction. In the research conducted by Justin Wolfers regarding the connection between money and happiness the study reveals that rich people have more happiness than less wealthy people. Countries that are wealthy have more happiness than countries with lower incomes. When we are satisfied with our wants, we're happy. For our wants to be fulfilled, we require money all the time. Do you remember the day when you had your smart phone, laptop car, or any other item associated with the joy you felt. As you look back on the day you were there, you will be reminded of the happiness you felt during that time. There is no way to arrive at the idea of money being the sole element that can bring happiness to your life. It is evident that if you're rich, it can bring happiness to more ways.

Experiences to buy

If you're rich, you are able to spend your money to experience new things that are connected with your joy. It is possible that you have met those whose love for their lives is traveling that gives them new experience. Travelers' lives are filled with experiences. Each day brings a different encounter for their lives. A variety of experiences can be a source of joy throughout their lives.

Photography is an alternative aspect of traveling. Photographers frequently take photos to keep a record of their trips and journeys. Of all the hobbies around all over the globe, photography has to be the most costly. Photography requires lots of your cash. If someone is looking for fulfillment in photography through an interest, then he will need to shell out a significant amount of money.

If you're not a very spiritual person, you require money to fulfill every desire that you have. It may be necessary to spend a less money however, sometimes it might need greater. The amount you spend will depend upon the quality of the learning experience you're gaining.

Purchase time

The most crucial factor for all people. There is a need for time to learn as well as to work, earn money, and also to have fun. It is essential to have money for these activities. If you're attracted by money, you need think about the fact that you must have the plenty of time for these crucial aspects of the world. If you're constantly involved working to earn cash, you'll be miserable in your existence. Also, you will not have enough time to attend to other matters throughout your day. It is crucial to remember that time is an important aspect that allows you to keep a balance between your finances and time for a life that brings you satisfaction

In other people

Are you aware of the differences between an investor as opposed to an entrepreneur? For a clear explanation, by using an example that is simple, the investor purchases a cattle in order to get calves and milk, while the businessman purchases a cow to kill it in order to get meat. In this example it's evident that an investor will make an investment with the intention of keeping it, while businessmen make a purchase in the hope of selling. They can be a source of revenue that is easy to earn.

It is possible to sell shares to anyone who is willing to buy them in exchange for an amount of money. The majority of people prefer to purchase shares at a cheaper price and then sell them for a premium price once they increase in value. When you purchase shares, that you then sell at a greater price then the difference in price becomes the profit you earn and is referred to as capital gain.

"Berk Shire Hathaway" is a company that manufactures shirts. The company's manufacturing was experiencing a dramatic decline. Looking to bring back the company, Warren Buffett bought it. However, he ended up being unsuccessful in his endeavor and the company was unable to continue in its production. However, Buffett managed to turn it one of the top business to invest in. Since 2008, a shares of the company have been purchased for $150,000.

The person referred to as Strawoos was involved with gold mining in California. He was however not very skilled in mining. Instead the man was making a fabric that was worn by experienced mining workers. The dress was dubbed Levis Jeans. If Starwoos were success in mining, Levis Jeans could not exist.

These tales are proof of the stories of success that investors have. This is why you can make investments in other people. Even if you're working it is possible to invest in investment based on the potential financial rewards that you could take advantage of in the future.

For completing tasks

Being productive is another means of making money. For success it is important to not waste your time. It is essential to make the most of your time to the best possible way to achieve your objectives and achieve financial success. If you're given the task to complete, make every effort to finish the task within the least amount of time because the longer you're involved in your work and the longer you're taking up your time.

Establish milestones, and follow through in order to achieve these milestones. Don't lose focus until you've reached these goals. Also, if you finish your work before the deadline and you are successful, you'll benefit by the time you finish and this could result in more money being drawn toward your.

Chapter 4: Ways To Save Money

Earnings is crucial to determine your wealth. It is also important to think about your savings for a clearer picture of your financial situation. There are a myriad of excuses as to why you're in a position to not save enough. However, if you desire, there's an option. If you're looking to make money and earning it, then you should also focus to devise strategies that will save you cash. The most effective methods of saving cash are listed in the following paragraphs.

Choose a bank that offers the money back

The choice of the best bank to put your money is, first and foremost. It's crucial to have some cash to hand. There is a chance that you would like to reduce your debt. It is possible to save some cash. If you select the best bank, it will help you achieve more than the goals you set. "Right bank" or "right bank" can be taken to mean a bank that returns well. This means you need to take into consideration issues like ATM charges, fees for overdrafts as well as the rate of interest for savings accounts. If you're able to choose one with a higher interest rates, with no ATM charges and zero overdraft charges, you're financially secure with the correct bank. If you're unaware of these benefits currently, you may call your bank to ask for the details. This way, you will know that you're working with the right bank that will serve you effectively. You can also request the list of any additional charges that a bank might be charging. Knowing your bank's details can aid you in determining whether or not you want to work with the bank you are currently dealing or switching to another.

In general you will find three typical charges for banks.

The Check Fee is The charge for each cheque you compose

Balance Inquiry Fee: The fee you pay for finding the amount of money that there is on your account.

* ATM Fee: charge you incur when withdrawing funds from a teller machine that doesn't belong to the institution where you hold your account.

Divide your paycheck

If the vast majority of your income is used for pay your bills at the moment it is possible to allocate the money in different ways would be something new to those of you. The trick is to share your paycheck in such a manner so that you don't have unneeded costs. It may be difficult for you to split your pay in the event that you're not used to doing it. However, the practice could help you over the future. Below is a an initial guideline the amount you may allocate to every section.

* 35% of housing costs Your mortgage, tax or renovations as well as other living expenses are included into account under this.

*15 percent for transportation costs: This includes car payments as well as other types of fees for transportation services.

* 10% repayment of debt Pay more for your credit card debt, and lower on student loans. The majority of the time the student loans will be less costly loans and can be used for extending.

* Save 10 allot money to the net amount of your funds.

* 25% for everything aside from medical procedures as well as food and other necessities This is the area where you should be most strict when it comes to

your budget. Pay attention to this. If you are able to cut corners every month, you may have the ability to allocate additional funds into your other expenses.

Create goals using a budgetand tracker application

Thanks to the advances in Information Technology and the software improvement, you are now able to track your income and expenses on a every month basis. When you have these apps installed within your mobile phone or your personal computer it is easy to track the expenses. You will have no reason for doubt as you will have an exact understanding of the cash flow.

Through these budget-tracking apps, you can establish goals and follow through. Some of the most used budget tracking applications comprise OneReceipt, Budget Tracker, ClearCheckbook, The Birdy, Check (formerly Pageonce) and TheExpenceTracker. They provide a background that allows users to keep track of their spending. A majority of these applications can be downloaded for free, and are offering a basic user interface. The charts and drafts created by these applications effectively show your financial situation, giving you an extensive view of your finances. They monitor your earnings and create budgets which make the process of financing easy for the user. The apps can also send you alerts in order to stay clear of late fee on your bills.

Verify your accounts

If you're having accounts, it is important to get into the practice of looking them up frequently to keep track about where you stand financially. This lets you know the time when funds are credited, and when funds are taken out. It keeps you informed about the current balance on your account. Once you have a clear picture of the amount of your account, then you have a better idea of managing your debit and withdrawals while shopping. This also shows you the way you can spend your money and control your spending. Today, a majority of banks provide the option of joining your bank account with your phone. Each time you conduct a transaction, receive a message on your phone. The service could be an time-saver for you as you receive updates on your account. It is essential when writing checks. This helps you understand the way you can manage the amount you spend.

Chapter 5: Establish The Skills To Manage Money

One of your main desires that you have had in your life was making a lot of money while having a luxuries life. If you think the money itself will do it is not the case, then you're sadly wrong. If you don't control your finances and manage it properly, you will not be able use it to improving your lifestyle. Thus, you should make a plan to control your money to make maximum value from your wealth. A few smart ways to save the money you spend are listed in the following paragraphs.

Take on the responsibility if you spouse is married.

If you're the sole breadwinner in your household, it can be difficult to handle every expense that is related to the family. It is at this point that sharing with your spouse will help you with your finances. There are now two people in the family. If there are two people within a group, it means that the financial stability of the family is secure. In the case of paying for your expenses together jointly with your partner are able to relax when you're earning.

In a few areas of the globe the husband can be the sole source of income for the household. It is believed that the family culture assigns them certain duties, as if a husband's role is to provide for the family, while the women's duty is to care for children. However, with the increasing price of living as well as the rise in inflation, women have also been compelled to work to support the family. If we look at the situation from a economic terms the catalyst is for attracting funds to the family. Both partners are accountable with regard to the financial issues in the family. Two sources of income can be very beneficial should a break need to be inserted in an income source, there's an additional source of income to protect the financial stability of your family. Sharing the responsibility on your spouse can be the best way to handle the financial burden.

Be transparent when learning the skills of financial management

It is essential to be honest in your development of financial management abilities. If you don't have sufficient knowledge about the financial management process it is possible to talk with those who can aid in this area. They can help you handle your finances as well as your debts, investments the purchase of a property, pensions, and insurance. If your earnings are going down, while debts are growing and your skills in financial management can help save yourself from financial disasters. If you're negotiating with your spouse about the cost of your living, it is important keep your communication open to prevent problems. If, for instance, you're sharing expenses with your spouse or if you both contribute to the flow of funds towards your family members, there must not be any hidden agendas. Particularly, if managing a joint bank account together with your spouse, both spouse should have a record of the account's every withdrawal and deposit. Each of you must be aware of the funds circulation. When a transaction occurs without knowing about it by another person that could affect the understanding between the parties. Be transparent and stay clear of these occurrences in order to remain financially secure.

Set up a budget for managing your financials

If you're taking care of your finances it is essential to establish an appropriate budget that allows you to handle financial issues financially. This helps you understand the financial situation you're in. If you don't create an established budget, you don't understand how much money you earn and where money goes out of your account. The ability to understand your earnings is the primary goal of creating the budget. Also, it will show you what percentage of your budget was spent on prior purchases of credit.

The process of establishing a budget helps to save money by creating objectives. If you've created your budget you will know how much you must keep from your paycheck for everyday expenses, and also the amount you need to reserve in the event of an emergency. You can, for instance, make a plan that each month you will allocate 10% of your earnings of your credit card. This serves as a way to remind you and also a tool that assists you in staying focused.

If you budget it is a sign of commitment to your objectives, even if you don't have the conscience. It outlines the way for you to achieve your objectives. Also, it can cause your savings to be triggered in accordance with specific objectives. This makes you more secure against immediate satisfaction and lets you remain focused on the goal. In this case, for instance, you're saving up money for an electronic device. Every month, you budget an amount of money from your budget just for that. If you use this money on something that needs to be done in a hurry it is likely you won't be able to purchase your laptop in date you scheduled. However, if you're trying to stick to a budget, and you are committed to your objectives.

The budget also provides you with the budgeted expenditure prior to the date of your budget. This way you can know the cost of your expenditure as you understand that should you make a decision to spend money that is not in your budget, it impacts your financial situation. It isn't possible to earn an endless amount of money. Budgeting properly helps you control your earnings while minimizing additional cost. It will alert you if you're planning to spend for something that is not within the budget, thus protecting your financial.

If you manage your financial affairs, and you create an budget, it will put you in the driver's seat. This places you in a place in which you control your money and not letting money control your. You are conscious that when you make a purchase in a reckless manner, it will have a devastating impact on you.

The budget you create aids in tracking the progress you make towards achieving your goals. Your budget ought to be a written document that must be consulted regularly. It will tell you the financial situation of your business and also the difference between it and your objectives. It will help you remain secure until you have reached your goals without losing concentration.

Make sure you assign all your financials and do not leave a dime in your account that is not designated

It is not a good idea to leave any penny that is not assigned. If you fail to give a price to the money you have, it will be exposed to unwise spending. In the event that you visit the restaurant, regardless of whether you give a service person a gratuity and you don't have to pay for it, you are able to add the gratuity into your dining price. If you decide to do that then you will realize the worth of your dollars. You will not regret wasting even a cent of the money.

Make sure you give an allowance as well as your spouse.

The allowances do not only belong to youngsters and kids. Everybody wants allowances, which makes them satisfied. If both of you receive an allowance in line with the amount of your earnings, it will be a delight for both of you. The amount could be as little as $5but it'll be a great gift to make you feel happy. Most important is that you must use this amount to satisfy some you "wants", not for "needs". You can't get the benefits of the allowance if you use it to meet an obligation at home. The money must be spent for a luxury item that will make you feel happy.

Learn about credit cards work and how they are beneficial in managing your money effectively

Credit cards is your most trusted companion or most dangerous enemy depending on how you use it. If you handle your credit card well, you can become a trusted friend that isn't pushing you to the debt trap. Credit card to pay for household expenses including gas and food and then pay them off at the end of each month, avoiding any additional charges or charges. The ability to accumulate points and earn cash back rewards can be a great benefit. To do so it is important to bear your eyes on the fact that these costs should be based on your budget for the month. It allows you to pay off your credit card balance at the close of your month. Don't utilize your credit card to make daily purchase. If you use the credit card and have an unfounded notion of the date it is due to be paid it is not a good candidate for credit card owner.

It is also forbidden to make use of your credit card to purchase items that aren't affordable. If you're not a position to purchase the item today, it's more likely that you won't be able to afford it in the near future, or at a later date. This is why you should be sure to leave no room for credit. Also, you must stay in the 30 percent your credit maximum. This is vital for maintaining an excellent credit score. Additionally, smaller amounts are easy to control. It is also important to examine your credit card statements carefully each month. Don't assume that the information on your credit card account is true. Unfortunate errors can occur at any moment. If you are confronted with a dispute or unauthorised charge it is imperative to report the issue immediately.

Chapter 6: Obstacles To The Attraction Of Cash

Possessing debts with a long-term repayment

If you have long-term loans, you're far from getting prosperous. Prior to applying for loans you must think of a variety of factors. You must determine if the loan is feasible for your needs. The reason you seek the loan is to meet your financial needs. It doesn't mean you're an unsecured debtor for the rest of your existence. A loan must be taken according to your ability and paid off in a short time. If you're dragging over the length of time it is also costing you the interest in a substantial amount to pay the loan. It is money that can be put to use in investing in a profitable way. Therefore, debt that is long-term can hinder your financial growth.

With outstanding amounts

If you've made someone a loan and they are required to pay you back in when. Nobody wants to give someone cash. Thus, even the debtors aren't going to be able to compel you to repay the money. You are on your own hands to remain on the phone with them until you receive the cash. If you don't, you're in danger of losing the money. If you are in debt arrange to receive the money quickly, leaving no time for delay.

Neglecting Duties

If you manage a business and you manage a business, you must fulfill some set of responsibilities. How you carry them out can directly affect the lure of funds. As an example, in the majority of shops the greeting cards are offered by consignment. If you're selling them, it is your responsibility to provide the cards, and then wait for an agreed upon time frame to earn the money. If you don't go to these shops and do not receive money at the conclusion of your time and you're financially deficient. Each employee's work is a factor in producing revenues. Thus, understanding each employee's tasks and responsibilities, and carrying out these tasks on time is important to make sure you are attracting cash.

Dependant on others

Dependency can be a major problem for earning income. It can make it hard to create a source of income on yourself. You may find that some business owners are highly successful who are unable to pay their bills in older years. One reasons could be the fact that they don't have the backing of their children in order in order to continue their business. If you are dependent on the wealth of your parents, it will be impossible to make room to inherit your riches. It is possible to enjoy your wealth the benefits of being rich.

However, if you have everything easily, it does not force you to put in the effort and make money. It doesn't create any the wealth you want, it simply reduces the wealth already exists.

Chapter 7: Daily Tasks To Help You Attract The Wealth

Write down the exact type of wealth that you would like to achieve

There are a myriad of methods for making money. If you're looking to earn wealth, it is important to recognize that wealth is available through a variety of ways. It is possible to start your own business and grow it to earn a decent income. It is also possible to make investment and earn a huge income. Rent your vehicle or house and earn cash with no worries. If you are contemplating the amount of wealth you require then you are able to create your own plan to attract wealth.

Pay attention to the potential of making money from people around you

Being vigilant can turn into the best investment you can make. If you don't know, you could be sleeping on an enormous wealth. Because of this, it will never earn you any cash. Finance expert and author Laura B. Fortgang stresses that people are inundated by wealth-generating ideas. However, only a few people can grasp these ideas. If you pay attention to the ideas that can create wealth that are all around, it can provide you with a substantial amount of cash. Perhaps you are worried about having an empty room within your home. It is possible to rent the room that is there and earn cash. It is also possible to donate used tins that you've thrown away to a company that buys metal. The same can be done for paper or plastic as well. This techniques won't make you millionaire. However, they are sure to appeal to the desire of the money.

Being gratitude

Every morning, write three things you're thankful for. If you establish it as an habit, you'll discover over your time that you're fortunate to have so many blessings to be thankful for in your life. A feeling of prosperity works mentally to bring money into your. A lot of people believe that they're poor because they aren't aware of how valuable their current possessions. Instead, embrace a sense of gratitude and you will attract prosperity to your life. Be grateful for the things you have in your life before thinking about things you want to own.

Set a date for your wealth-attraction plan

Make a list of the sum of money you want to earn in a given period of time. This can help stay determined to achieve your goal of the success you desire. Set milestones, and meet them while sticking to your deadline. Make sure you set realistic objectives so that you have the likelihood of meeting these goals. Convince yourself that you will succeed in achieving your objectives by doing the tasks immediately.

Chapter 8: Think Out Of The Box

The majority of people believe about the same routine ways to make cash. The only way they think to earn money is getting to work in the early morning all day and then returning late at night. This alone can make you tired. If you take a different approach to thinking, you could make a way that will lead you towards a viable source of earnings. Many people have earned their money the direction of innovative ideas.

A man's story about how he gained his wealth by stealing the Iguana

An individual decided to adopt an iguana for pet. His wife was not too interested about the manner in which he took the animal. A few days ago, she inquired from him if he would be able to earn some cash just playing with the Iguana. He embraced the question as an opportunity and considered ways to earn some money from his beloved pet. So, he decided to publish a memoir about his pet iguana. He entered "iguana" in Google. He was able to search those who were interested in the Iguana, and to create links for these people.

He then created a questionnaire of the challenges facing those who suffer from Iguanas and then consulted with a vet. He was satisfied that the veterinarian addressed all of his concerns. After that, he wrote an ebook that was made accessible for purchase online. The book also stated that he will also be publishing the sequel to this publication under the name "Iguana Story Part II" that will reveal the secrets to Iguanas' lengthy lives. The second edition was much costlier than the original book, and the pages were also smaller in comparison to the book that was first published. In his book, He mentioned that protein is essential for well-being. However, the iguana is called vegetarian. So, where do people get Iguanas' protein? You can now understand why the people who needed to consult the author to find out. In the direction of a vet, he created special foods and brought it on the market. Today, he has a full life.

Filmmaking

The majority of you have seen the film "Pirates of Caribbean". Anywhere this film is shown across the world the director Walt Disney is getting paid. Then, not only him, but its principal actors Jonny Depp as well as Keira Knightley too are money in the same way. Since it is an art form, art, it is essential to think creatively and with a sense of humour. If you've had the luck and luck of being an actor in a film, then you are also able to have an opportunity to earn income in the field of film.

The writing of a book

The writing of books is another method to be rich while also accumulating money. The writer of "Harry Potter", J. H. Rowling became one of the wealthiest individuals in the United Kingdom by wring books. There are so many things we experience through our daily lives. If we could communicate them through the medium of writing, we may turn it into a income stream. People's experiences differ from one individual to the next. By sharing your experiences with others, they can inspire themselves to learn from their experiences and gain knowledge.

For a start, you could engage a ghostwriter. As you browse the web, you'll find that there are many ghost writers who work on freelance web sites. They write pieces with copyrights. Many publishers are publishing their works by this manner.

You can work online

Today, we live in the world of Google. The way of life for individuals has changed significantly. Dressing up in formal attire isn't the only method to earn money today. Working online is rapidly increasing in popularity due to the speedy advancements in web hosting. There are numerous benefits to becoming freelancer. You are the boss of your own business. When working in an official job, you need to attend the workplace in a formal dress. If you are working online it is possible to complete your job while sipping an iced tea in the comfort of your the comfort of your home. The best part about working online as a freelancer is that you can choose your own preferences as well as what you are able to become more professional in. In traditional work there are times when you must do what the manager tells you to perform regardless of about whether or otherwise. It is not a fixed pay when working online. Based on your skills and commitment the amount you earn can be increased. It's a great method of making money on your own.

Chapter 9: What You Need To Do To Make Your Costs Standstill

You can cut out expensive items from your budget

Everybody wants to be a part of the luxuries of life. However, if the cost of living is greater than the earnings you earn then you will never live living the lifestyle you want to live. Know your finances and make the appropriate expenditures. Reducing expenses on luxuries can help enhance your financial health. If you change from an extravagant lifestyle to one that is more simple, you could experience a dramatic shift in the way you live your living. This can be a fantastic method of saving cash. There are many ways to live a more simple lifestyle, that will increase your financial stability. As an example, you could remove yourself from the optional TV or internet subscriptions. Also, you can be thrifty in choosing the best package for your mobile. Selecting a low-fuel automobile that is easy to maintain is a good way to save your cash. If you own any electronic devices that aren't being used, trade them in and earn cash. In some cases, the same product can be found in several stores and at various prices. It is all dependent on the name of the brand. To find out more it is possible to visit a thrift shop.

Consume less

If you consume a healthy diet and eat well, it will not only improve your financial standing as well as your overall health too be better. The majority of people will spend their money for food, but they are able to make a great dinner at home and save money. If you're planning to eat in a restaurant, the best option is to avoid going on your own as it's extremely expensive. Large restaurants usually offer discounts or special deals for meals purchased at a huge quantities. Choose healthy and inexpensive food items instead of buying expensive processed food. It is important to understand that eating healthy is typically more affordable. Stores selling groceries on a large scale provide discounts when goods are purchased in large quantities. It is possible to take advantage of its benefits and save dollars. If you frequently go out to eat, now is the right time to put an end to this. Make it a habit to cook at home, instead of heading out to restaurants every time you want a dinner.

Cut down on your energy use

The excessive use of energy eats up the wealth of your household too. If the monthly bill for electricity exceeds your budget it is time to think about methods to save energy. There are a variety of strategies that are easy to follow in order to cut down on energy use and reduce your expenses. Switch off the lights while you're not in the room. If you are leaving your office or your room, switch off the light switches. Don't use a/c If there are alternative sources that can make the weather more favorable for your needs. Open the doors and let cool air through. If it is cold, dress in appropriate clothing, such as blankets, oats or other special heaters that can warm you up. The investment in solar panels is the most economical method to ensure allows you to reduce your electric bill.

Utilize efficient transport methods.

These days, many people lead extremely busy lives. There is always a need to go on trips. If you are traveling and have a comfortable mode of transportation, you'll be spending a significant amount of cash. If you're a regular person who travels, it is possible to make use of public transport. In most major cities, you can find subway, metro or street car lines running within the cities. In towns that are mid-sized there are trains and buses accessible for use. Most of the time there are special transportation packages provided to daily travellers. Transport for office workers can be seen as an efficient method for travel. If you live close to your office, biking or walking could be an option. This also allows people to breathe in the fresh air while exercising prior to going into the workplace.

You can have fun and not waste money.

The average person spends a significant amount of money on entertainment. A few people are completely in debt due to spending a large amount of money on the entertainment. If you make the right choices you will be able to cut down on expenditures on entertainment, and have the ultimate liberty of living. Eliminating unnecessary luxuries from lifestyle is a great way to save the money. Fun doesn't suggest that lots of cash has to be thrown away for it. It is possible to have fun without spending a dime. can be found in drinking a cup tea with the closest person within our lives. This isn't about the amount of money we spend, but the psychological fulfillment we experience that counts.

Reading becomes a great way to enjoy for a lot of individuals. Additionally, it's less costly than videos and films. The saying goes that it is reading that makes you a better man. The same way, reading is a great way to get satisfaction you've been looking for. Many avid readers enjoy reading with a great deal of pleasure. Reading regularly enhances your life.

Being with friends and having fun, and doing activities for free is also budget affordable. Together, you could play a game on the board and take a ride on the bicycle or visit a region of town you've visited before. They could cost a minimum of funds or not even. Thus, you will have ample opportunities to have fun together with your buddies.

Beware of addictions that can impact your financial situation

Certain habits are bad that will drain your money in an instant. Many of these behaviors can result in health problems also. If these behaviors are ingrained throughout your life they can be very difficult to stop them, without assistance. In removing these dangerous behaviors from the beginning and avoiding them, you will be able to save the cash in your bank and your overall health.

It is a terrible habit to engage in. If you're plagued by smoking cigarettes regardless of your conscious you will spend an enormous sum of money each day in order to quit. Some regions in the globe, cigarettes can be quite costly. They not only cost you dollars, but also deteriorates the health of your body. Drinking regularly can be the flip side of the side of the coin. Additionally, it can have negative impacts on your health, based upon the health condition you are suffering from. In the long run, a drink addiction can result in a huge expense. Cocaine and heroin are among the most damaging aspects of the tale. They can affect your well-being as well as your financial standing. If you are looking to end those addictions to improve your financial well-being You can speak to an advisor and receive support.

Chapter 10: How To Spend Your Money Smartly

Your goal should be to make lots of money and living a full life. However, earning abundance doesn't mean you will succeed until you make wise use of them. Certain people earn a great deal and then end up in debt for not investing the money in a smart way. Real rewards of earning cash can be enjoyed if spending money in a wise manner.

Prioritize first to the most essential elements

There are needs and desires for everyone. The first most important thing to do is your basic needs like food, home and clothes. Food is an essential need. For those who prefer eating out at an elegant restaurant is something you want. The need for cloths is an absolute. But wearing costly clothes to create an attractive appearance is something that everyone wants. The need to travel for their regular choruses is an expectation. Yet, the most expensive transportation option for comfort is an absolute necessity. If you are able to put aside on your essential needs first and wants, you will have more money to meet your needs. If you reside in a house that you rent the rent should correspond to the family size. If, for instance, your property is too large for you, then you're spending a lot of dollars.

It is your second most important goal to save your emergency fund

If you do not have a savings or emergency account now is the best ideal time to create one because it allows you to be able to live comfortably with a large amount of cash in your account to cover an emergencies. This gives you protection of your finances in the event that you go into an unforeseen situation in which you are unable to make any further. So if you're covered by an insurance plan for health, the first priority is to pay your insurance monthly. If you budget, it's crucial to establish funds aside for an emergency reserve.

Remember to repay the debt

If you do not manage your debts, they can dramatically influence your financial standing. The minimum amount you pay for loans could prolong your period being a debtor. You can save money over the long run and can help you get free from debt more rapidly. It is also an excellent idea to settle your debts, including an interest rate that is high. This is a highly efficient way to save cash. If you don't, you're spending a lot of cash as cost of interest. When you've set aside sufficient funds for your essential requirements and an emergency fund, you are able to allocate a certain amount of money towards the repayment of the loans. If you're applying for a loan, make sure you opt for a plan that offers the lowest interest rates. If you take out a loan from an unofficial lender You can always bargain with the lender or offer you with the best interest rate.

Make some room to save

In the next step, you must save some funds to save. If you've established an emergency fund as well as cleared your debts or you've just about paid off all of your debts, then you should make room in your savings also. It is crucial to keep your funds in a bank account that can multiply your savings. If you're choosing an institution, be aware of the interest rate they offer as well as other advantages. If you've got an account for savings it is not advisable to withdraw your savings account for purchases you make on a regular basis. It is important to maximize its benefits in the long term. Experts recommend to begin saving when you are in your 20s, and set aside minimum 10-15% of your earnings to savings.

If people are paid or get their wages it is common for them to be compelled to buy something on impulse. You can prevent this from happening by putting money into savings accounts immediately after they are paid. In order to make this easier You can also bargain with your boss to transfer some of your earnings into your savings account once you get your paycheck. It is possible to do this through setting up an automated transfer system with your bank. This can help you reduce your expenses without much exertion.

The ability to be smart, not essential are equally important.

Once your savings have been accumulated there is a little funds left. This could be used to invest the funds to make an investment, which could not be as significant as food, clothes and other requirements. However, it should be designed to bring benefits in the future. As an example, you could purchase an ergonomic chair to your workplace. While it's not the primary requirement to have however, it allows you to sit for long periods at the office and not suffer from back problems and can yield you profits. Another example is when you are required to spend all day at your computer while at work, then you should consider buying an eyeglass that will be comfortable to your eyes. This will enable the user to sit for long periods of time. It will also lead to increased performance. It is possible to apply this idea whenever you purchase something, taking into consideration how they is connected to the financial health of your family.

Luxury at the very

The luxury items aren't in"needs", but rather to "needs", but in the category of "wants". Saving money shouldn't necessarily suggest that you must lead a tough existence. If you don't experience luxurious lifestyle, then we cannot call it a satisfied lifestyle. The luxury of life is not a requirement that make you feel comfortable, satisfied and secure. So, they are required in your life to provide their satisfaction. Based on the amount you earn each month it is possible to spend your money on spending money on luxuries like eating out at expensive eateries holidays, the latest vehicles, new cable TVs as well as expensive devices and more. These kinds of activities are excellent methods to get rid of the monotony of your daily routine and rejuvenate your lifestyle.

Chapter 11: Money And The Root Of Evil

The issue of money affects the lives of everyone in one way and in another, hundreds or hundreds of times per daily. It is an important influence on your life's vibration as well as in your own points of attraction. If you're in control of the things that influence the majority of your day and you are able to control it, then you've accomplished an important task. The majority of your thoughts throughout each day revolve around the issue of money. If you're able to focus your mind on this issue and make it clear that your financial prosperity will increase, and this prosperity will improve everything else in your daily life.

It's interesting to note that while light travels at a speed of 800 miles per second the thought can travel at a rapid pace. Thought is more refined than energy, which is the mainstay of electricity.

If you're looking to make your own life, and you want to control the way you live your life, your understanding of topics of money, the beliefs you hold and patterns of thought are crucial for you.

IT'S ALL ABOUT ENERGY

Energy is the main topic. Everything physical is composed of the vibrations of energy. Life, successes, our ideas and our joy, our opinions ... all of it has to do with energy. All of us are made up out of the energy ... small molecules that vibrate at a specific frequency. The energy of this vibration is the basis of our existence.

All things are made up out of energy, and it's the energy we continuously use to attract everything in our lives.

Thinking patterns that repeat emotions and feelings create impressions on your subconscious mind. The thoughts you think about then become your thoughts and beliefs, which then begin to resonate in your mind, pulling from the Universe the reality of your life, individuals who are in your life, situations and even events which match your frequency. Be aware that your thoughts are the real force behind them.

There is more power in your life to make it what you think. Your life is being created right now by your ideas and thoughts you choose to believe. They're the primary factors in determining your reality and deciding the course of your future. Your beliefs and thoughts are your most powerful power within your own life and you control completely!

Also, it's crucial to understand that there are many types of energy or levels of energy this is the reason that can make everything interesting. Positive energy is a magnet for positive events. Positive energy draws negativity to situations.

Positive energy wards off negativity while negative energy stifles positive circumstances.

If you're depressed, you'll draw negativity and negative individuals to your life. Also, you'll be able to block out positive events and individuals.

In contrast when you're feeling positive, you'll be attracted to positive circumstances and individuals. Also, you'll be able to avoid undesirable situations and individuals.

If you're not receiving what you desire, it's likely that you're not transmitting the correct vibrations. People detect your energy vibrating on an unconscious scale. They do not know how but they feel it as a sensation or feeling around your. All things happen in the subconscious, however, it begins in your conscious mind. Your beliefs and thoughts determine your energy levels and create your vibrational energy. Your thoughts and ideas send messages to your subconscious mind that radiates your level of energy (the exact energy others can detect). Your beliefs may be helping you, while others are oppose your beliefs. There is no truth or belief that is in absolute. It is possible to alter any belief that is unpopular and build another one. You are able to pick the beliefs you believe in. Nobody can make you believe something Only you decide on which beliefs you want to be a part of.

It is true that you can make any kind of the reality that you desire by changing your thinking and belief system.

Positive thinking and positive belief generate positive energy. People who have positive energy draw positive events and events happen to them. they get to meet amazing individuals and have fun. When they keep doing this it naturally makes them more positive. They make positive choices and continue to draw more and many positive individuals, circumstances and things into their lives.

"Matter is the shape that basic experience takes when it comes into your three-dimensional system. Your dreams, thoughts, expectations, beliefs and emotions are literally transformed into physical matter."

If you're surrounded by doubt, negative thoughts, worries, doubt, and the feeling that you're in general won't ever improve, then you're releasing thoughts that only draw additional things that you do not wish for, as well as more anxiety or self-doubt and will make you think that the situation will never be able to improve or work.

It's a viscous loop and if not properly broken, will just result in worse situations.

How do you alter your mindset?

How can you generate positive energy that allows you to are able to enjoy positive experiences?

"Everything is energy and that's all there is to it. Match the frequency of the reality you want and you cannot help but get that reality. It can be no other way. This is not philosophy. This is physics." ~ Albert Einstein

THE CONSISTENCY OF THE LAW OF ATTRACTION

Every aspect of your life, and your life of the people in your life are affected through your Law of Attraction . It's the reason behind every manifestation you can see. It's the foundation of all that you experience. your awareness. Everything is merely a part of your life. You draw it every single one of them. There are no exceptions to the general rule.

It is said that the Law of Attraction is responding to your ideas and convictions every moment of the day, therefore you can say you create your own realities. There is no one else who is able to influence whatever you want to attract, except you. If you are focused on negative things and focusing on it, you're creating the environment. It is inviting undesirable things to enter your life by paying concentration on them.

For a better understanding of what is the Law of Attraction better, think of you as an attraction, attracting your attention to what you feel, believe and believing. If you imagine a thought of something you would like to have the thought becomes larger in size, becoming becomes more and more powerful by your belief in the Law of Attraction.

The Law of Attraction remains constant and constant throughout the Universe.

Keep in mind that all vibrations are and it is the Law of Attraction responds to these frequencies and arranges them by bringing objects that have similar vibrations to each other while retaining those frequencies which aren't similar.

It's easy to identify the type of vibrations you're generating, since you are in the Law of Attraction is bringing the evidence to keep you on track of the vibrations you're making.

If you're drowning in the anxiety of lacking the financial sources you require to make it happen, or even the possibilities that could bring money remain elusive ... and not due to the fact that you're unworthy or not worthy, but due to you are not worthy. Law of Attraction can only be applied to things that have a similarity but not items which are different .

The more comfortable you are more comfortable, the higher your attraction point be and the more positive the outcomes for you. If you're feeling poor the only things that make you feel like poverty could come to you. When you're feeling wealthy the only things that appear as if they are prosperity may come to you. It is the Law of Attraction is consistent If that you are attentive, it will show you, by observing, how it functions. If you can remember that you are the results of what you focus on and observe the results is happening - then you are on the right track for a happier life.

Because you are aware that the Law of Attraction is always in response to the energy you send and transmitting, it's important to recognize that your thoughts let you know if you're on the verge of making something that you would like and would like or you don't want.

It is also possible to speed your creation process by paying it greater time and the Law of Attraction takes care of all the other details and will bring your what you're contemplating.

If you are looking to boost the power of your magnet, it's crucial to be aware that thoughts you have with no powerful emotion are not going to hold much magnetism. Each thought you make does have power however, it's the combination of thoughts and powerful emotions that is more potent.

WHAT IS VIBRATION?

Everything has a vibrational basis. Every time you hear something you interpret vibrations into the sounds you hear. The sound you hear is an perception of the vibrating. Every physical sense of hearing, seeing as well as tasting, smelling and even touching are present because all of the Universe is vibrating. Our physical senses read the vibrations. They also provide us feedback on the vibrating.

Every thing that we see in the air, the water, dirt as well as in our bodies is a motion of vibration and is handled through the Law of Attraction .

The emotions of our bodies, the most potent and vital of our six psychic interpreters of vibration, offer us continuous feedback on our thinking, as the thoughts we think about are linked to our emotions.

The world that is not physical is made up of vibration. (Thoughts and Emotions)

The world you are aware of is vibrating.

Nothing exists beyond vibratory energy. It is impossible to find anything that cannot be controlled with The Law of Attraction.

FEEL ABUNDANT AND ABUNDANCE WILL MANIFEST

If you can make a comparative between what you've been feeling and thinking about and your experiences within your own life, you're able to start making adjustments to improve your quality of life. If you're not making this comparison and you continue to make up that you are not capable of doing what you would like your desires are likely to remain unattainable. Many people attribute power to external factors as a way to justify their reasons for not being prosperous for example: "I'm not prosperous because I was raised in an unsuitable environment. I'm not wealthy because so and so has cheated me or because I'm not worth it, ..." therefore I could go on and on. The story that of never having getting rich.

And I'm here to inform I want to tell you that your "not prosperous" because you vibrate at levels which is different from the amount of wealth. It is impossible to feel low and feel poor, yet become prosperous. The abundance and prosperity you seek cannot come to your vibration unless you're radiating abundance and prosperity.

There is no way to respond to the realities of your life only to change the reality. Find a way to experience the thrill or joy of knowing what your wanted to achieve before your desires can be realized. Discover a method to visualize your ideal, be able to feel it, and to ensure that the vibration you create can be in line with the dream or wish. If you could create a sound of your dream prior to the manifestation, then you will be able to manifest the dream you have or wish.

In order to transform your lifestyle and achieve your goals, you need start telling your story how you would like to see it, and not think the past or the way it's been ...this is vitally important.

You must expand your thought process beyond the limitations of so that you can attract an alternative or something that is different and.

CHANGE YOUR STORY

In order to change the way you live it is necessary to consider your thoughts with a clear mind and, in order to achieve this, you must understand what to think. There is only one thing to begin doing, which is sharing your tale in a different method. It is essential to present it in the way you would like to tell it. Once you have started recounting the tale of your life, which that you always do through your thoughts as well as your words as well, you must to be comfortable as you share the story.

Every moment, in anything, you could decide to concentrate upon the positive or negative. When these choices show them to you, then it is your choice to choose between paying attention to what you desire or not in the event of. If you are able to tune into your thoughts, emotions and the way you feel, you will be able to discern which option you're at present focusing on, and you are able to alter the way you think about it often.

Today, there's a trend for everyone to speak the truth regarding what's happening within their own reality (tell the truth as it really is) instead of making the declaration of your desires. Be aware that this won't help you as it will not alter the way you see things. It is necessary to tell an entirely different story if wish for to use the Law of Attraction to bring the things you want! !

One of the most effective ways to tell your brand novel story is to pay attention to the words you're doing in the present If you find yourself at the center of something that's not in line to your ideals then stop, and tell yourself "I am aware of what it is I don't wish to have. What do I really want?" Then deliberately make the declaration of your desires.

I'm not happy with the reliability of this vehicle.

I'm looking for a brand new, solid automobile.

I'm fat.

I would like to slim down.

If you focus on the subject of your choice and affirming that it will become what you wish that it will be in the course of time, you'll experience the change how you feel about it that indicates a vibratory change.

As your frequency changes the point of your attraction alters as well as your manifestation point. It is impossible to talk about what you would like and want without the Universe giving the core of that to you.

"You create your reality according to your beliefs and expectations; therefore you should examine these carefully. If you do not like some aspect of your world, then examine your own expectations"

FEELINGS

It is important to clarify to make when you speak in the language of what you wish to achieve, and simultaneously you're feeling doubtful of your thoughts, then your words do not bring you the results you are looking for, since your way of feeling will be the most accurate indicator of the direction you are taking your frequency. It is the Law of Attraction is not reacting to your words, but to the sound that is being generated by you.

But, as you can only discuss one subject at a time, you must choose to talk about the things you really want. If you continue saying it as you would like the outcome to appear, you'll eventually (and it won't be for long) modify the balance of your sound. If you say it regularly enough, you'll begin to feel the words you say.

Physical existence is a way for you to discover and comprehend your energy. Its transformation into thoughts, feelings, and emotions, is the source of every experience. It is a fact that there are no any exceptions. - Seth

YOU ARE A CREATOR

You are the one who creates the things you see within your daily life. It is crucial to realize that it's not your actions, or your actions or what you're declaring, but rather through the thoughts you are generating. The first step is through the thoughts you're making.

There is no way to talk or perform an action without a mental thought happening, however, you may have thoughts but not take action or speak phrases .

Each thought you have is a unique vibrational sound. Every thought you think of either comes out from your mind, or regardless of whether it's something that is influenced by another or if it's the result of what you've been thinking or someone else is considering - any thought you're thinking about at the moment is resonating at the frequency of your own, as well as through it's Law of Attraction that thought attracts thoughts that are its Vibrational Match. These thoughts, when combined, have a frequency greater than any thought before it; the thought can now, thanks to their own Law of Attraction , attract an additional thought and yet another thought, until your thoughts become powerful enough to draw attention to a real reality' scenario or manifestation.

Everyone, everything like events, situations, and people can be drawn to you due to your thoughts you think or thought. If you can recognize that your thoughts are making things happen and reality, you can discover an ability within you to control your thoughts.

When you begin to direct your thoughts towards the direction you would like to and you begin to feel more and better as the energy generated by the improved sensation and thoughts will become close to the frequency of what you would like to achieve.

If you decide to concentrate upon a specific aspect of someone or something who you dislike You are placing you out of vibrational align with the things you want.

When you experience a powerful desire for something, or have a intense interest, these are times that are in complete harmony. If you are feeling more positive, the more at peace with your desires and goals.

In contrast the other hand, if you feel unhappiness, it means that you're not in sync with what you desire.

Think about "What do I want?" After that, simply switch your focus to the thing you would like to achieve. When you focus your attention on your desires then the attraction that is negative will cease; and then it will be a positive one. Additionally, at that point the negative feelings will shift to a feeling of happiness.

It's important to be aware that you are getting whatever you put your mind to whether you desire it or not. Law of Attraction is always constant. So, you're not just telling the story of what is happening now. Also, you are writing the tale of the possible future you're making right now.

"You want something, you dwell upon it consciously for a while, you consciously imagine it coming to the forefront of probabilities, closer to your actuality. Then you drop it like a pebble, forget about it as much as possible for a fortnight, and do this in a certain rhythm." - Seth

HOW TO FEEL BETTER RIGHT NOW

I am aware that it's simpler to be focused on positive things if they was already taking place in our daily lives. If you think that you are only able to have the capacity to concentrate on events that are happening and what is taking place isn't pleasant and you are unable to wait for all your life due to the fact that your focus on an unwelcome issue is keeping desired things from happening to you.

It is not necessary to wait around for the perfect event to occur within your life to be happy. It is possible to set your focus on better things regardless of how you feel about your day-to-day life.

The things that enter your awareness are taking place as a result of your frequency. The vibration you receive is a result of your thoughts. contemplating, and you are able to discern by how you feel which thoughts you're having.

Be aware that if you fixate on an unwelcome thing trying to get it out of your way but it's going to move closer to you, as you are what you pay attention to, regardless of whether it's something you would like to have or not.

The world we live in is an Universe which is built upon "inclusion." There is there is no "exclusion" in this Universe. If you come across something you would like to have and you decide to affirm it in reality, you're telling yourself, "Yes this thing that I desire and want please come to me." However, if you spot something you don't desire and are shouting"no" to it, you're actually telling yourself "Come to me, this thing that I do not want."

Within everything in the world around you, there's something you would like to have as well as that which you do not want. It's up to you to be focused on what's desired. Your mind is powerful, and you've got more control over the events you experience than you think.

When you're feeling down and you're trying to attract an object that is not pleasing to you. The reason you feel negative is that you're focusing on something that you don't desire or the absence of what you want.

Do not view negative feelings as an unwelcome thing, instead look at it the negative emotion as an crucial guideline to determine the direction in which you focus...and your direction of vibration...that will determine your direction and the results you attract.

An additional aspect that is important to comprehend is the difference of "wanting to feel good" as well as "not wanting to feel bad." This isn't the same thing. There are two ways of saying exactly the same thing. These two statements have the exact opposite of each other, that is why they have so many different vibrations.

It's also crucial to keep in mind that any thoughts you're thinking about, whether it's some memory, something you're observing right now or looking forward to in the near future the thought you are focusing on is circulating within the present moment, and is drawing attention to other thoughts and concepts with similar thoughts.

Your thoughts not only draw attention to other thoughts like them however, the longer your focus is on these ideas more intense your thought becomes and the greater attract power they gain.

The attraction you are attracted to comes in the daily things you're thinking about, while you move through your day. You can direct your thoughts either way or the other.

Your thoughts are brimming with potential for creativity and attraction that is only tapped by consistently focusing on things that feel great. If your thoughts whirl around between unwelcome thoughts and things you want it is a loss from the constant flow of positive thoughts and remain where you are.

THE LAW OF ATTRACTION ADDS POWER TO THOUGHTS

In many cases, when we are faced with something that isn't ours and are faced with a dilemma, we want to justify why the situation has been happening, and attempt to prove the reason for being in this circumstance. If you're defending the situation, justifying it, or blame anyone or anything that you remain at a point of negative attraction. Whatever you do, while explaining the reason you are not experiencing how you wish you to experience, can further increase the negative impression, since you can't focus on your goals when you're explaining the reason the situation is one that does not suit you. There is no way to concentrate on both a negative and positive one simultaneously.

If you try to pinpoint the source of your problem in the first place, you just keep you in that negative trance for a longer time. Recognizing that something's not what you would like the situation to go is an essential stage, however once you've identified the issue more quickly you'll be capable of turning your focus towards an answer and the more successful. Be aware that the issue has not the same frequency as the solution.

If you feel uncomfortable regarding something you are thinking about or talking about something that you'd like to change - for example, a healthier economic situation or better relation or physical state it is a moment that you are preventing yourself from achieving an improvement.

Chapter 12: Attrac Money And Manifest Abundance

For many people, financial freedom and wealth are two things that go hand-in-hand. Financial freedom doesn't have to be an arduous one. It doesn't have be a huge amount of physical or mental effort because I'm going guide you through in easy-to grasp terms, how you can make the most of the energy at your disposal. I would like to demonstrate how to differentiate between what you've had about money and how you feel while contemplating those thoughts, as well as the flow of money through your life. If you can discern the difference and then determine to make your decisions according to the comparison, you'll gain access to the ability that is the Universe and discover that time and physical exertion are not essential in your success with money.

We'll start by saying "You get what you think about." or "What you think about you bring about."

Most important to know in order to enhance your financial position is Money involves two aspects:

1.) money, lots of money, a feeling of security and peace the abundance of money may provide as well as

2.) the lack of money or not enough funds feelings of anxiety and dismay caused by the fear of not having enough of money can bring .

When people say"I want money" and "I want money," they're talking positively about money. However, if you're speaking about anything, even money, and are in a state of discomfort or anxiety it is not talking about and focused on the issue of having enough money but instead on the topic of insufficient money. It is crucial to distinguish between the two since the declaration brings emotions and money, while the words are keeping it in reserve.

It's important to be aware of the thoughts you're truly thinking and most crucially, how you feel regarding money.

If you're thinking or thinking: "Oh that is a very beautiful thing - but I cannot afford it," you're not in the right place to allow the wealth you desire and want to see. A feeling of sadness which you feel when the realization that you are unable to afford it indicates that your mind is pointing toward the absence of what you desire rather than your desire. Your negative emotions that you experience is just one method of understanding your thinking as well as the result you're experiencing are another method to determine.

If you're experiencing a financial crisis and you're aware and talk of it regularly then you are in a negative situation. Therefore, use your authority and share your tale about your financial situation in the way you would like you to tell it rather than what it actually is. not be honest about what's going on.

If you look at the world around you and think of the things that are, you will be unable to achieve the results you want. If you wish to see significant changes in your life, it is essential to give distinct vibrations. That means you have to think of thoughts that make you feel different while thinking about these thoughts.

"Tell me what you believe and I'll reveal how your life is. You can also tell me.

What is your ideal life and then I'll share with you my views."

ACTIONS

Anything that comes in a state of desperation will always be counterproductive and will eventually cause an impression of being lacking . That feeling of being unfulfilled you feel isn't satisfied by taking action, since your feeling of being lacking comes from the frequency of discord between your needs and your daily routine of thinking.

Thoughts that help you feel happier by telling a new story and looking for positive things can help you fill feelings of being deficient. Once this is done then the things that you've always desired will start to appear into your life. They will come to you due to the fact that your sense of inadequacy has disappeared.

It's crucial to keep in mind that if you decide to take action with to achieve satisfaction, you're taking it in the wrong direction. Make sure to direct your thoughts and words to the things that help you be more comfortable and happier after you've reached a level of satisfaction amazing actions will be motivated and amazing outcomes will be the result.

If you don't spend the time to align your thinking then more actions is required, but and not yield the same positive result. If you're taking action at the moment, and not taking an action that brings you joy but doesn't lead to happiness It is against what is known as the Law of Attraction . Instead of being eager to act to achieve what you desire and want, you must first look at them in your mind, imagine them and then expect that they'll come.

If you only look at the present and what happens, there is no way to make things better for the better for you. It is essential to find ways to be optimistic about higher things so that you can see any improvements on your behalf.

If you're experiencing feelings of being in a state of battle, this is due to the fact that you always comparing where you stand today in relation to what you're trying to reach. As you keep taking scores by observing the distance you remains to be covered in order to reach your goal, you just increase the distance, the work as well as the exertion which is the reason the reason why you feel like it is it is a battle.

If you're contemplating a future destination it is easy to exaggerate your feeling of disconnection between the place you currently are and that final destination. That way of thinking does not just slow the development of what you're making however it also keeps your creation apart from the rest of you forever. Your thoughts are the attracting factor of your life. When you take the time to discover thoughts that make you feel great, you'll place yourself in the position that is attracting you and the things you're looking for will arrive faster.

It is essential to discover the nature of your desire prior to the specifics of your need can become apparent to you. It is essential feeling more successful prior to more wealth coming at you.

If someone is lacking regardless of the amount of effort they make, is likely to attract the feeling of more desperation. Lack's powerful effect surpasses any actions you offer. Anything that comes in the context of a feeling of desperation can be detrimental. In the absence of any feelings of need, there's none and the actions will be productive.

I'd like to I ask you...How are you feeling each time you make your payments? Are you fearful? Are you feeling the sensations of being not wealthy enough or feeling disappointed? The thoughts that come to mind are negative thoughts about the topic of money. Without realizing that your main thoughts regarding money have been focused in the unsatisfactory part of money instead of the abundance part of the money.

OTHERS' ASSESSMENT

The opinion of others about you is not a factor in the quality of your life If you're not awed by their opinion. The comparison of your own experiences with those of others may intensify the feeling of inadequacy if you reach an assumption that others have achieved more than you did in the end, which triggers inside yourself the feeling of feeling "less than."

Additionally, noting the lack of success from the lives of other people doesn't put you in a position that you can attract more prosperity for your own life, since you'll receive what you are thinking about.

The things you attract to yourself or do not keep away from you is not in any way connected anything else anyone else is doing. A more positive feeling of wealth regardless of the fact that your actual situation doesn't support the belief, always brings an increase in your wealth. Be aware of the way you feel about money can be a effective way to be more successful than looking at what others are doing.

In order to allow more money into your lifestyle requires only a very little effort. It is all that is needed is achieving an equilibrium in your thinking. If you are looking to make to make more money, but are unsure if you are able to achieve it, then you're not in harmony with your goals. If you're looking for more money however you believe there's something wrong with you being richer, then you're out of the balance. If you are looking for greater wealth but feel angered by those who have more, then you're not balanced. If you're experiencing feelings of feeling inadequate, insecure and jealousy as well as insecurity, anger, and more, you're out of sync to your desires.

There is nothing more crucial than feeling good about yourself because if you're having a good time, you're at peace with the things you want. If you don't let go of the emotions of struggle, the things you wish for will never be the reality of your life.

WHAT'S YOUR STORY?

An attitude of lack is the primary reason why more and more people aren't giving themselves the money abundance they want. If you think there's not enough money for everyone as a result of the fact that more than others of it that you're holding you back from having the wealth which is yours. The other person's level or success that's the cause the lack of success you have and not your own negative perception as well as your focus on the absence of your own desires.

The things that anyone else is not has no bearing on your experience. All that matters to your perception is how you utilize Energy by focusing your thoughts.

Your wealth or deficiency of is only a matter what you see from a particular perspective. It is all to do with your thoughts that you think. If you'd like your energy to change, you need to tell a different tale.

If you are critical of those who are doing in a healthy way, it may be indicative of your poor habit of thinking. The focus on lack exacerbates the feeling of lack wherever you go. Your constant criticism in your mind will only serve to keep your vibration in discord with the things you desire.

If you feel negative feelings on any topic, it suggests that you're experiencing an idea that you're currently battling by other ideas.

Discord in your vibration is the main basis for the negative feelings. Negative emotions are a sign that your thinking patterns don't align with the current goals you have set.

Focusing on the negative opinion of other people will never be effective because it causes discontent within you. It will also hinder the manifestation of positive thoughts. There will always be those who don't like you and paying concentration on their opinions will make you feel like you are in conflict with what you want to achieve. Be aware of your emotions and pay attention to the way you feel so that you can determine whether your choices are appropriate as well as your actions. Be confident in yourself and be sure you are in control of your feelings. When you feel at ease, you're at a point of being attracted to the things you wish for.

DOWNWARD SPIRAL

A major reason that causes anyone to go through a downwards spiral is due to the attention paid to what's not. Because you are afraid that you might lose things, or paying concentration on the things that your losses are causing the focus becomes on the absence of something you desired, and so you keep that as your focus, just the possibility of losing more is there. When you find yourself feeling smug or frightened, or you start to rationalize or excuse or blame or blame others, you're in the negative side of the equation. Only further lack could be the outcome of your reality.

When you reach the point where you are at your lowest and have nothing to loose, you mind shifts, and so does the vibrations. Your experiences been through in life led you to want lots of wonderful things coming to you. However, your anxiety and doubt, fear and anger, blame or jealousy or negative emotions is a sign that the thoughts you're thinking about hold those thoughts back. You've been attracting them to your home however, your doors are shut. When you start telling an entirely different tale, and as you relax and think about the positive aspects of your life choosing the best emotions, the door will become open, and you'll be filled with things you would like and wish for.

Be aware that paying attention to what you don't have you'd like can cause it to grow and become closer the same way that focusing on what you desire causes it to grow and be closer towards you. If you feel as if your financial situation has become an issue, you're moving your financial situation further However, once you begin to relax regarding your financial situation and your finances, you're allowing an abundance of wealth to come into your life. This is as easy as it gets.

Recognize that what people make with their money is not a factor for the way you think, and that the most important thing you can do is contemplate, talk and perform the things you feel comfortable doing and you'll be attracted to abundance in all areas that you live in.

THE MOST IMPORTANT SKILL

One of the most valuable skills can be developed is the ability to direct your thinking towards what you would like and paying the full attention you can to it. It's an incredible capability to control your thoughts, and produce outcomes that are not comparable to the results that a single action will yield.

It's crucial to understand that you do not need to have money in order to draw wealth, but you can't experience poverty and then attract money. What's important is that you need to discover ways to change how you feel exactly where you are, prior to things starting to shift. If you shift your focus from what is not working and telling stories that move towards the things you desire Your vibration will begin shifting, and your focus of focus will change, and you'll begin seeing different outcomes. Find reasons that make you make you feel happy. Find what you are looking for to achieve and keep your mind at a point that makes you feel great.

NEGATIVE FEELING

The only thing you get is what you imagine. If you're thinking of the absence of money you're experiencing the deficiency of cash. The manner in which you feel while you think about your thoughts if you are attracted to the positive or negative aspects of what you're thinking about.

The Universe doesn't take no for an answer. When you're saying"No, I don't wish to live in poverty, paying attention to poverty means that you are saying, Yes Come to me with this kind of poverty that is not what I want.

Whatever you pay focus to can be a call for the manifestation of that. If you declare"I want money" but you cannot get it the attention you pay to the absence of it is equivalent to telling me, come to me the absence of money which I am not interested in.

If you're thinking of money and you are feeling positive in your head, the thought comes to mind. If you're thinking about money but you're experiencing unhappiness, you're keeping it from happening to you.

THE STRUGGLE FOR MONEY

A lot of people think that it is necessary to put in the effort to be successful and at the end, they'll get rewarded for their efforts However, this does not align to The Law of Attraction ; you will never have a satisfying conclusion to a miserable travel.

If you are of the opinion that you need to be a hard worker to earn money, then you will not come your way unless you put in the effort.

It is important to remember that the amount of money you earn as a result of physical actions is not much when compared to what is generated via alignment of the mind.

It is not possible to have negative thoughts about something but then try to make up for the negative thoughts with actions or work. If you can direct your thoughts, you'll realize the full power of Energy.

You create your own real-world. What you focus on. There's no other primary law.'

SHORTAGE

Are you aware of the sensation of being in a state of desperation? The feeling of being in a state of deprivation can slow the flow of adding more money into your account. If you find the notion of making money a hassle, I'd suggest not to make purchases while being afflicted by the sensation of anxiety. Anything you do when you're experiencing negative mood isn't an ideal choice. The cause of your feeling of discomfort does not lie in the act of spending your money, rather it's a sign that your ideas regarding money at the moment do not match with your desires.

Believe that everything that you wish to receive is there to you. All you need to do is accept it to be a part of your daily life. Your experiences of being in a state of deprivation do not arise because you have no enough resources available however, they are due to refusing to allow it into your daily life.

"You receive the blessings from the gods. You make your world in accordance with your beliefs. it is your creative power which creates your reality There are no limits for the self, except the ones you are a believer in. "-Seth

CHANGE YOUR POINT OF ATTRACTION

We all understand that it is impossible to reverse time to erase all negative beliefs, there's nothing to try, even if you wanted to as all your power lies in the current moment.

When you discover a feeling which makes you feel happier this moment, your point of focus begins to shift...NOW! The reason you may appear as though negative thought is affecting your current life is due to the fact that you've had negativity and negative thinking throughout your life. It is an idea you keep to believe. The belief itself is only a belief pattern. However, you are able to try, even just a bit and start a new one, tell the story in a different way, to get a new vibe and to alter your focus of attraction.

"From healing from disease to the span of our lives, and our success in careers and relationships, everything is perceived in "life" is directly linked to what we believe." Gregg Braden

The Spontaneous Healing of Belief

Keep in mind that you are in the Law of Attraction is responding to your energy and not the actual reality that you live However, if your energy is focused solely on the reality you live it will never change. Change your frequency by imagining your ideal lifestyle and focusing your mind to those images until you experience relief this will signify an actual shift in vibration took place.

If you start telling an untruthful story when you begin to tell a negative story, your Law of Attraction will help you to look beyond your current viewpoint, to the past and even your future. But the same pattern of lack will remain. If you dwell on the being in a state of complaining, you create an emotional point of focus which allows you to access many more negative thoughts, regardless of whether you're focused on the present, your past or the future. Your story you tell yourself will set the new patterns of your thoughts as well as shift your perspective towards attraction. A simple act of searching to find positive qualities from where you currently are can set an entirely new tone of vibration that does not just affect how you feel at this moment but start to attract the people, thoughts, events as well as things that are appealing to you.

"Feelings are emotions that react to the beliefs.'

Chapter 13: The Law Of Attraction Expand Thoughts

It is said that the Law of Attraction says that anything that is similar to itself is attracted . Also, what is thought to attract to it other thoughts similar to it. This is the reason that when you're thinking about something which isn't pleasing, thoughts of more negative ones attract your thoughts. You also have the capability of focusing on your own thoughts and your life and on things which matter to you. The ability is there to envision things that will happen in the near future, or events which have occurred during the past. when you approach it to find interesting things to consider and discuss it is possible to quickly alter the way you think.

"Imagination and emotions are the strongest kinds of energy that are yours. A strong emotion can carry the same amount of energy as for instance, the is required to launch spacecrafts into space. Seth Godin -- Seth

YOU DO HAVE ENOUGH TIME

If you don't understand how powerful your mind and don't take the enough time aligning your thought patterns so that they can be a source of power you're left to create using the power of your decisions that, when measured against others with others aren't very effective. It is possible that you feel like you don't have enough time to fulfill the goals you have set. However, I would like you to realize that when you connect in harmony with your Energy of the Universe through the power of focussing on your thinking, you'll create an advantage that allows you achieve things that been previously thought to be impossible even quickly.

You can do anything that are not able to be, perform or accomplish once you've set your mind and focus in the right direction. Prior to things manifesting the proof of your alignment will be in positive emotions. According to the Law of Attraction says: Anything that is akin to itself is attracted. Whatever you feel - you're attracting even more of that to your life.

When you have a desire or want some thing, be confident and trust that you will succeed in achieving the goal. If you have a desire and you are unsure the sensation of doubt can be the sign that you are not going to never achieve it.

It is possible to go the place you're currently at towards where you'd like to go, but you need to understand that what is happening "now" is just an area you're at. There is a fast way to get towards things that you like. You must be focused on the direction you would like to go - not on where you currently are, or else you'll never get there. your goals. It's important to keep in mind that you can't make up your mind outside of your opinions.

When you concentrate your focus to feelings of lack, weakness and powerlessness, it creates an increase in feeling powerless and vulnerable. It is impossible to focus on overcoming the poverty issue without paying the attention you need to the issue of poverty. It's crucial to start being grateful for what you are able to appreciate and begin changing your attitude. It is a hectic time and have a lot to think about. In this way, we place our self in disarray and poor is the consequence. Then you dwell on money insecurity and continue to suffer from a financial insecurity. You can end the cycle at any point.

"As far as you are concerned the present is your point of action, focus and power, and from that point of volition you form both your future and past. Realizing this, you will understand that you are not at the mercy of a past over which you have no control."

It is hard to stay away from thinking about poverty, or the absence of income when you're experiencing it as a reality. The majority of us do not consider what we would wish for until we live things we would rather not live. We tend to drift through the day, wandering around and there without thinking about our thoughts with any real awareness. We don't fully grasp the impact of our thoughts we tend to not think positive thoughts until confronted by something that does not suit us. When we find ourselves in a situation that isn't what we like, we take it on with all our might. We then give it our focus, which makes the situation even more complicated. When you're living suffering from poverty and worried about finances, search for thoughts that don't feel like worry and concentrate on these feelings.

There must be an effective way to separate the events within your life and your emotional response. That is, you could be experiencing the middle of financial difficulties and feel fearful however, you could also feel in a similar situation, but feel optimistic. Your situation doesn't have to determine your mood or what you're contemplating. There is a possibility to consider something different rather than worrying about money. If you manage it, then the situation will be better. But if, once your situation arises and you pay it full attention, you'll create an even greater amount of the things you would rather not have. It is clear that your habit of thinking triggered your financial problems but to change into a positive outlook isn't likely to take a long time as you are now faced with the burden of anxiety and stress to manage.

In situations when you feel anxious, there are instances of more and less anxiety. Select the most positive emotions. If you keep reaching to thoughts that provide emotional comfort, the positive thinking will bring you back into a positive place.

If you're experiencing any other than abundant and prosperity, you have the vibrations of resistance. The reason for resistance is that it's based on what is not happening. you want. It is caused by the focus on the things that are wanted. The resistance you have to face led to poverty at the beginning as well as the resistance you have to poverty is what holds it back when it's present. Attention to the things you don't desire that causes undesirable situations within your life, so it's logical to pay focus on what you wish to achieve would be a good idea.

At times, you may think you're thinking about money however, you're really concerned about breaking. One method to know the difference in vibration is taking note of the emotional state that accompany your thought process.

Set a goal for your self to feel happy, and guide your thinking in the right direction. You will discover that, without even realizing it that you've been storing up resentments and feelings of inadequacy and feeling helpless.

Every person is accountable for their thoughts as well as the objects they select as their subjects of focus.

Be aware that the world around you unfolds right now and can be seen in the way you are feeling right now. If life seems difficult as well as unfulfilling and difficult This isn't due to being not in the right place and your outlook is distorted by thoughts of contradictory ideas.

You could see this as the start of your journey - trying the best you can to avoid negative emotions, and resisting the negative thoughts about your worthiness, or feelings of resentment which surround the financial situation - you will changeimmediately!

Make a list of the things you would like to achieve.

List things that can be pleasant about the place you are.

You should be excited by the new improvements which are coming to you.

Don't stress what you don't dislike.

Focus on what you enjoy about your job.

Be aware of the universe's reaction to your increased vibration.

Chapter 14: Appreciation And Gratitude
The definition of appreciation is that it does not include resistance. When you're in the sate of gratitude and appreciation you are not afflicted by doubt or anxiety. With the feelings of appreciation and gratitude, you don't be a victim, and you will just feel happiness. If you are focused on the things that you would like and then describe the way you envision your life be, you'll move towards

emotions of gratitude and appreciation. As you begin experiencing the sensations of gratitude and love that will pull your attention to all the things you believe to be beneficial and powerfully.

If you're not grateful for the things you've got then you'll never be able to get more. Spend time focusing on the things you've got and be grateful for your possessions. It is the constant state of being thankful and grateful.

"The every day practice of gratitude is just one of the ways to increase your gratitude.

Wealth will be yours." Wallace Wattles

Set yourself the goal to select objects that grab your eye and instantly inspire you to be grateful for them. It is essential that you begin to work on the higher frequencies. When you are focusing on the things that make you feel good about you, the simpler it will be for you to keep having a good feeling. If you continue to maintain these positive feelings, the greater you are able to attract the Law of Attraction will deliver to you ideas, feelings as well as people and objects which match your energy.

It should be your primary goal to look for things you be grateful for throughout the day. It is the strongest link between yourself with the Universe. The process puts you in the position to enjoy more success throughout your life.

As you develop gratitude and appreciation and gratitude, the less resistance can experience in your energy. In addition, the more resistance you can overcome and the more positive your experience is going to be. Furthermore, once you practice gratitude and gratitude, you'll get more comfortable in the sense of having an increased vibration. This means that you'll notice that your vibrating isn't as high.

When you discover something you like more, the better it feels as well as the more enjoyable it feels and the more you'd like to take action; the more you try it, the more satisfied you will experience.

The Law of Attraction assists you in generating the power of your positive feelings and thoughts to the point that, in a short amount of energy and time, you'll achieve the state of feeling grateful.

Even if you do not know any information concerning The Law of Attraction or you do not even believe in it The practice of this method will help you to be connected with the power of the

Universe All desires you have are likely to come into your life.

If you're in a state of appreciation and gratitude, you will feel absolutely no resistance in your energy. Keep in mind that it's your own resistance that sets your from what you desire and want.

If you're in the feeling of being grateful it is actually raising your frequency of vibration to let what you've desired to manifest into your life. When you appreciate, you're inviting what you desire and wish to manifest into your life with ease.

It would be beneficial to allocate between 10 and 15 minutes per daily to complete this task. When you begin to focus on seeking out things you cherish and appreciate You will notice that your life is full of such aspects. The feelings, thoughts and emotions of gratitude and admiration come naturally.

When you are able to appreciate or praise someone, each moment you are happy over something, you're seeking the Universe to give you additional of these. If you're at a place of gratitude and appreciation, then all goodness will be flowing into your life. Keep in mind that if you wish to feel gratitude and gratitude, you'll be drawn to something that you be grateful for.

When you're seeking reasons to be thankful and happy about, you're in the power to control your own energy and the source of attraction. But in the event that you're reacting to how others appear to think about you there is no control over the way you feel. When you're more concerned with what you think about yourself than in how people perceive you, there is more control you can exercise over your own life.

After you've decided that there is nothing more crucial then feeling happy and have determined that you'll find something you take note of, what is the focus of your interest has turned into your feeling of gratitude.

YOU CANNOT FEEL TWO EMOTIONS AT ONCE

All that influences your life is how you're vibrating. This isn't about luck either luck, chance or. If you're looking to raise the vibration of your life, appreciation as well as gratitude are the most effective and fastest method to do it. When you are focused on appreciating the moment, your appreciation will come back.

The life you live isn't only about the past or future but rather about the present today. It is all about how you're creating your Energy!

" The intensity of a feeling or thought or mental image is, therefore, the important element in determining its subsequent physical materialization ."

- Seth

It could be challenging to find items to be grateful for. The following exercises can help you draw certain people, events and events to your life. This will significantly and quickly increase your chances of creating the life you've always wanted. You'll also feel better after you've completed the exercises.

Maintain a gratitude journal every day

Each day, take 5 to 10 minutes each day to record the things you are grateful for in your day-to-day life:

Example:

Monday the 17th of January 20...

I'm happy that I wasn't scared today

I'm happy that I've less thoughts of negativity today.

I am grateful for having a an active and healthy body

I'm happy to feel less anxious in my body.

I value my friends.

I'm grateful to work.

I am blessed to have an roof to shelter my head

I'm thankful for the opportunity to eat three delicious meals per day.

Etc.

This way, you'll be able to be able to clearly assess the amount of improvements you've already made and motivate you to continue your progress as you continue to improve.

Chapter 15: The Duality Of Money

One of the principal ideas I have to debunk is that of the notion that money is either beneficial or harmful. It is the foundation for a number of our long-term beliefs that want to make to accumulate more wealth is an indication of greed. It's an intrinsically evil or a weak characteristic to have. There are many more beneficial philosophies could be embraced to achieve financial wealth while maintaining a more optimistic perspective.

In the final analysis the concept of money is merely an idea that is not real. It does not exist or have any basis on the ground. Nation A states that it's responsible for exports of X amounts and imports Y from other nations, and consequently the value for its money is Z. This is substantiated by the value of currency from other countries floating around the vaults that are electronically linked to the nation A as well as the quantity of gold stored into its banks. They, using the identical gold, create sheets of paper that feature prominent men printed on their fronts--each sheet of paper illustrating just a tiny fraction of gold as well as the currencies of different nations. Because the value of gold, the worth of the currencies of other nations as well as the worth of the currency in question are all decided by individuals, without any inherent significance of their own, they're digital figures. These virtual sheets of paper that have artful doodles or drawings on them could either be positive or negative. There is, however, plenty of it available to be used multiple times. Like I said in the beginning, the reason that wealthy people earn greater wealth than the rest is due to their understanding of the meaning of the concept of wealth.

The concept of wealth rests upon money, however in a distant and in the end, unimportant way. The connection between money and wealth is the same regardless of whether you cook the porridge using wheat or oatmeal. Although the taste of the porridge might vary, the fundamental idea of the recipe is similar, and so is the final product, which is the healthiest carbohydrate distribution method. The same way prior to the advent of currency and barter was introduced, there was a barter system. In those days the principle that underpinned wealth was exactly the same, even though its nature differed. In the end it's just the tool used to achieve get to the end of the road, with no significance in its own. If everyone stopped using money in the future and began trading only in oxygen tanks, will it make oxygen tanks better or bad, or perhaps permanently crucial? They would not be so important. Their value will be just for as long as their place within the economy.

Wealth is, however can last for many years and is longer-lasting. As it's an abstract concept Let me try my best to bring this to you. Wealth represents liberation from having to have money, rather, having it used to accomplish your next phase of lifetime goals. The wealthy do not get up at dawn trying to survive however, they're earning additional funds to meet their longer-term objectives. Be careful not to think that rich people aren't concerned about having $200 or $2000, or even 20k in their bank accounts. Their basic requirements are cut down until the very last detail and their needs don't change after they have become millionaires. In contrast to those who want to invest their money when they earn the money, people who are wealthy are only willing to alter their spending habits in the interest of their longer-term goals. And to them, money is nothing more than the vehicle driving them to their final destination-achieving their dreams. There is no greater power than the gas in your car's tank with the capability to grab and hold the wheel.

If you've listened to my reasoning up to now, you'll discover that there's a strong perception of ambiguity about the importance of money within the concept of wealth. One hand everything depends on its existence in the framework of. But, on the other hand there is no significance outside of its existence. Consider this: A person holds you in a guns and warns that if you don't comply that he'll shoot at you. However, he then states that he'll shoot at you in the same way regardless of how long. Do you really have a reason to refuse with everything you have? No, right? The same way the money you have is there or it's not.

There's no need to worry about the availability of it or its scarcity because it's never within your reach. But, it doesn't alter the way you view the idea of it. If there wasn't money and you were free from the shackles of money, then freedom could allow you to earn a little.

If there is money the case, that freedom could allow you to create much more. To achieve this liberty, you must learn the techniques to manifesting it and apply attractivity to get the most of it. You'll have to master and apply those mental habits of those who are wealthy. That's the topic we'll be discussing in the following chapter.

Chapter 16: The Attitude You Need To Adopt

One of the first things that successful people realize is that it's okay to chase cash every time. The bizarre attitudes that society has towards almost insanity-free morality regarding financial endeavors solely for the sake of money's motives is the major reason that most people don't attain sufficient funds. But, if the stockbrokers earn profits and are willing to accept promotions solely for the purpose of earning more, despite their dislike for their job, they'll continue to be able retire millionaires when they reach 35, and follow their interests. Therefore, there's no harm in pursuing the money for a time, when it can help you reach your goals over time.

Wealthy individuals reject the notion of morality based on money, because they know the fact that morality will only be spread through individuals' use of money but not through it in itself. This is something you must understand also. Don't be enthralled by the world of money and stop looking at solely as if they're beneath bigger and more noble concepts. Who is nobler? Entrepreneurs who took advantage of every chance to make money, then retired at the age of 37 and lived the rest of his existence giving to the cause and striving for his own goals in life? or the perpetual middle manager in an office who snubbed every opportunity since pursuing money on its own was not his thing, and he could not give as much to charity since he didn't have the money and lived his whole life living in debt with his basic ideals still in tact? You decide.

Another area in which wealthy individuals are very different from people that are poor or relatively well-off or the simple fact that they are rich, is the way they view their the needs and wants. If you've noticed, those who spend their money and enjoy making the appearance of being rich they are, rarely remain wealthy for a long time. The people who have a comfortable lifestyle may have been more prosperous if they changed their views on desires and focused on essential needs to a certain extent while their income was growing. At the opposite end on the other hand, there are plenty of low-income people with decent sources of income periodically however, they choose to utilize the money to pay for their immediate necessities, before they think about the long-term development of their finances. This is not the case for all, or all of them, but there is a substantial portion of these.

People who are wealthy tend to address their wants and needs only if they're the last of their priority items on their list. It's it's not the case all often. Instead, they put their cash into two realms of financial investment: the first is longer-term investment options, as they let their funds increase on its own within a short years without the need for constant managing. Additionally, as deposits and savings that are liquid into their growing savings accounts.

If money remains in the banks, wealthy individuals don't see any need to disturb it, or even spend it just because it's in the bank. The reason is that they might have additional possibilities for growth in the near future, which could need every penny accessible to them. While they are waiting the growing liquidity assets are also used as buffers between them and their debt. Are you aware of people who come from old-money families that still have the money they had? They tend to live more simple lives and tend to be very humble, despite the fact that they lavish their friends who surround them with loads of luxury. Bill Gates alone, who is probably the one who has spent more than any other person living today, is the perfect example for the people in this group. When wealthy individuals encounter problems, difficulties or other difficulties that are a part of their lives the wealth they accumulate are barriers that stop their downfall and help them get to their feet easy.

That brings us to our following point -- wealthy people dislike the idea of having to take on debt. They are aware that individuals are often faced with situations where they are required to incur the burden of debt via loans in order to finish the details of a plan that could lead to your goals. When this happens they consider the loans and debts as a detestable obligation and burden. They do their best to get rid of the credit before deciding to use every penny of the money they receive for their own. Wealthy people know more than everyone else the burden of debt and loan is a noose that impede their future growth in their finances. They don't want to choose to take on these obligations in order for the sake of enhancing their temporary lifestyles or even to entertain their naive or unimportant needs. It is a shame to borrow money for less important needs or empty wants, that could easily been avoided and is an incredibly frightening idea to those who are.

They're also much better at distinguishing between desire and necessity that the average bear. If you own a good outfit regardless of whether they're slightly shabby, but you're looking to build up the amount of money you have, buying that costly dress is a wish but not a requirement. Only when your current collection of clothes is ruined with a few holes, and that situation could impact your career or appearance at work and at work, will spending cash on new clothing turn into a necessity. And even after that, there's no reason to spend a lot of money on the most expensive of them. If your transportation needs can be met with an uncomfortable, but efficient and affordable public transport system There's no reason to borrow money to purchase a brand new vehicle right now. It's best to wait until the point when there's no need to consider the price of your car two times, and even less, to take out a loan for the car.

Another reason why wealthy individuals stand out from the rest of us is the fact that they are never in doubt about whether they're rich enough or likely to become rich enough in the near future. In no time do they think about whether they be able to afford their future plans. Instead, they view money as a game. They calculate the sum of the money needed for their dream to come to fruition, and then discover methods to get that quantity, and just implement those strategies to make sure they possess enough. Are you lacking a million dollars in order to realize your certain-fire success of your dream? Find the money, make your plan, talk to banks or sites such as Kickstarter and get the money (if the plan you've created is properly developed) then implement your the plan. That's it. This is what you'll need to take care of should you wish to learn and be a part of the laws of attraction to create wealth. Stop being scared of this thing.